# Embracing Encaustic

## Learning to Paint with Beeswax

### By Linda and William Womack

Embracing Encaustic:
Learning to Paint with Beeswax
Copyright © 2008 by Linda Womack and William Womack
Hive Publishing

Hive Publishing, Permissions Dept.
5417 SE Stark St., Portland, OR 97215


Author: Linda Womack and William Womack
Editor: William Womack
Book design: Lightbourne, Inc.
Cover photographs: Linda Womack

Manufactured in Canada

2nd Edition
1st Printing, April, 2008

10 9 8 7 6 5 4 3 2 1


ISBN: 978-0-9816774-2-2

LCCN: 2008926006

DISCLAIMER: THE AUTHORS HAVE MADE EVERY EFFORT TO INSURE THAT ALL INSTRUCTIONS GIVEN IN THIS BOOK ARE ACCURATE AND SAFE, BUT THE AUTHORS EXPRESSLY DISCLAIM ANY AND ALL LIABILITY, OF WHATEVER TYPE, WHETHER DIRECT OR CONSEQUENTIAL, AND HOWEVER ARISING FROM USE OF THIS BOOK. IF YOU ARE PREGNANT OR HAVE ANY KNOWN OR SUSPECTED ALLERGIES CONSULT A DOCTOR ABOUT POSSIBLE ADVERSE REACTIONS BEFORE PERFORMING ANY PROCEDURES OUTLINED IN THIS BOOK. THE TECHNIQUES AND MATERIALS IN THIS BOOK ARE NOT FOR CHILDREN.

# Contents

# The History of Encaustic Painting

*Enkaustikos*—the word means "to burn in." Three thousand years ago, a few enterprising Greek shipbuilders discovered a new use for the beeswax they used to caulk hulls. By adding pigments for color and resin for hardness, they created a painting medium with an unmatched depth and luminosity. Before long, encaustic art could be found everywhere, from painted ships to depictions of everyday life on urns, even applied to statuary to render a lifelike glow.

Encaustic painting weaves in and out of art history, gaining prominence for a time, only to recede into the shadows for centuries.

A thousand years after the Greeks discovered it, painters in Egypt resurrected the medium, crafting exquisite portraits to decorate the mummies of their patrons. In the seventh century, veneration of a Byzantine icon made of beeswax, with the ashes of Christian martyrs for pigment, was credited with saving Constantinople from a Persian attack.

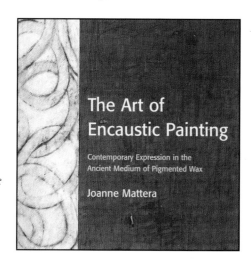

The Art of Encaustic Painting

Contemporary Expression in the Ancient Medium of Pigmented Wax

Joanne Mattera

The modern resurgence of encaustic began in the early 20th century. Mexican muralist Diego Rivera began painting with the medium in the 1920's, and in the 1950's, artist Jasper Johns further popularized its use. Two important exhibitions of encaustic work bookended the 1990's—*Contemporary Uses of Wax and Encaustic* in 1992, and 1999's *Waxing Poetic: Encaustic Art in America*. In 2001, Joanne Mattera's book *The Art of Encaustic Painting* brought awareness of the medium to a wider audience.

Funeral portrait of a bearded man. Encaustic wax painting on beech-wood. Egypt, Roman period, 125–250 CE. Location: Musee des Beaux-Arts, Dijon, France. Photo credit: Erich Lessing / Art Resource, NY. Art Resource Image Reference: ART130195

The popularity of encaustic painting is showing no signs of slowing, and in fact is only gaining momentum in the 21$^{st}$ century. It's no wonder we keep revisiting this ancient art form—few others can match its versatility, both in technique and result.

Wax is immediate; it allows no time for pondering. It's workably elastic only for the precious few seconds between being lifted from the hot palette and cooling on the board. Encaustic rewards *doing* over thinking.

For all its urgency, wax is also reassuringly malleable. If you don't like the way the work came out, scrape it off and try again! Heat it, let it flow, and it will solidify moments later into a new shape. Encaustic is the soul of forgiving.

As you will see in the following pages, works of encaustic can be sedate and smooth, or seductively dimensional. The wax has an inviting surface that begs to be stamped, gouged, and carved. It invites the viewer not only to look, but to touch and smell. Encaustic is sensual.

So get some wax under your fingernails and explore the magic of working with this uniquely expressive medium!

**Kevin Frank, Still Life with Blue and White Vase**

2004, Encaustic on wood panel, 20" x 28"

"I draw an outline of my subject, in graphite or charcoal, directly onto the panel before sealing it with encaustic medium with a tint of color. With the under-drawing visible, I block in the mass tones, alla prima, using straight encaustic paint with no medium added. I make adjustments to the form by using several metal tools including a small, spoon-shaped cuticle-pushing tool, which I usually heat first and a small pocket knife for scraping and incising. Sometimes to achieve more subtle shading, I use my thumb or forefinger to blend the tones. Typically, I use hog bristle brushes for large areas and small sable brushes for the fine details."

the sky is cool,

the deep heart's core.

**Judy Wise, Hearing**

2007, Encaustic, acrylic paint, paper collage, tarlatan on wood panel, 6" x 4"

"I under-painted in acrylic, then glued down a small piece of tarlatan, the bird image and the text. After adding wax, I incised lines and dots into the surface with sandpaper, a rotary tool and a round object. I rubbed oil paint into the incisions to finish the piece."

## Basic Supplies

In encaustic painting, beeswax, resin and pigment are layered to produce a deep, translucent surface that captures and reflects light. You can paint with wax alone or collage other materials into it, but you must fuse each layer with heat after applying it.

All artists have their favorite tools, but for basic encaustic painting you'll need:

- **A rigid support**—luan or birch wood work well.
- **Hot palette**—A pancake griddle, skillet or crock pot keeps the paint liquid while you work.
- **Encaustic paint**—you can mix your own or buy it professionally mixed.
- **Metal tins to hold the paint**—tuna or cat food cans work well.
- **Natural bristle brushes**—hog bristle brushes from a hardware store will do fine.
- **A heat tool**—a heat gun, propane torch or quilting iron to fuse the paint to the support.
- **Scraping tools**—ceramic and paint scraping tools work well in wax, especially when they are made of metal.

That's it! There are many more tools to try, but this will get you started without breaking the bank.

# Painting & Fusing

Start with any hard, porous surface. Wood panels work especially well, but stretched canvas alone is not sturdy enough and may continue to stretch with the weight of the wax. If you really like to work on canvas you can always stretch it over a wood panel to increase the support. I prefer to work on birch panels.

**The basic steps are paint, fuse, and repeat.**

1. **Paint** a thin layer of encaustic medium or encaustic paint onto your surface using a natural bristle brush. The wax will cool quickly as you move the brush, so dip it into the melted wax often to keep the brush warm.

**2. Fuse** the wax to the surface by slowly moving a heat source, such as a heat gun, from side to side. You must reheat every layer of wax after it is applied in order to fuse the current layer of wax to the one beneath it. Move the heat source in a circular motion to help remove any air bubbles.

**3. Repeat** these steps, adding encaustic paint, oil sticks, or collage materials for color and texture until your painting is finished. At any point in this process you can collage other materials into the wax, including dried plants, natural fibers, and handmade paper, or scrape away wax revealing the layers beneath.

## Buffing

After your finished painting has cured for 48 hours it should be buffed with a soft cloth to bring out the shine and make the wax more translucent. Repeat this step every few months or when the surface becomes dull.

# Terms

As with any art form, knowing a few basic terms will help you get started more quickly. A resource list of where to purchase these products can be found in the *Resources* section at the back of this book.

**Beeswax** is the basic element used in encaustic painting. I always use 100% beeswax, which comes in either natural (yellow) or filtered (clear). I prefer filtered beeswax as a neutral base for mixing my paint, but often the natural beeswax on its own gives a beautiful antique yellow tint. Other types of wax can be added in small quantities for varying effects.

**Damar Resin** is a natural tree resin extracted from the sap of an Asian pine tree. Please note that damar resin and damar varnish are not the same substance and are not interchangeable. Use the type that comes in crystal form.

**Encaustic medium** is a mixture of beeswax and damar resin. The resin is added to the beeswax to make the final surface more durable. It also raises the melting point so there is less chance of the wax softening in extreme heat.

**Encaustic paint** is a mixture of encaustic medium (wax + resin) and colored pigment. You can purchase encaustic paint ready-made or make your own. This is covered in more detail in the *Choosing Paint* section.

### Remember:
Wax + Resin = Encaustic Medium

Wax + Resin + Pigment = Encaustic Paint

# Tips & Tricks

**Always use 100% beeswax** because it is archival and will remain flexible. Paraffin or candle wax alone are too brittle and may crack with age.

**Beeswax comes in different colors.** *Natural* beeswax contains pollen which makes the wax yellow, *filtered* beeswax is clear.

**Keep it clear.** I usually begin my paintings with two layers of clear encaustic medium. That way, I can always scrape the painting back to a clean board if I'm unhappy with what I've done. Think of it as painter's insurance!

**Working with wax is very forgiving.** If you make a mistake or change your mind, you can always melt or scrape off the part you dislike.

**Acrylic and wax don't mix.** Generally these two mediums don't work well together, though some artists have had some success. Try oil paint, gouache or watercolor instead for a better chance of success.

**To break up a large block of wax** freeze it for 20 minutes in a plastic bag, then hit it with a hammer while still in the bag. It will shatter into smaller pieces, making for quicker melting while still giving you the reduced expense of buying it in larger blocks.

**There's no need to clean your brushes!** Just let them harden when you are done painting and soften them up on the griddle the next time you heat your wax.

# Warming Paint

Crock pots or fry pans are often used for melting large quantities of encaustic medium. Of course, once you use these tools for wax don't cook with them!

You can use a regular pancake griddle to heat smaller pots of encaustic paint. Use metal cans to hold each color and a separate brush for each pot. Some artists prefer to use smaller brushes and clean them when switching between colors. To clean your brush, melt a little paraffin or soy wax in a tin or directly on the griddle, saturate your brush and wipe it off with a rag or paper towel. Keep repeating this process until you no longer get color to come off of the brush.

### Containers or Griddle?

Some artists mix all of their colors directly on the griddle, while others use separate containers. I do both. There is no right or wrong here, use any method that makes the most sense for how you prefer to paint. The shallow metal caps that come with professionally mixed paint can make a nice container for small amounts of specialty color as shown here.

**Kimberly Kent, Fall**

2006, Encaustic on Claybord™, 5" x 7," *(cropped to fit page)*

"The underpainting was done in very thin layers of oranges and yellows and fused flat. I mix the colors directly on a tacking iron which acts as my paintbrush. Using an iron allows me to make both hard and soft edges, and the tip is great for linework."

## Applying Wax

Hake brushes are preferred by many artists, but even the cheap hog bristle brushes from a hardware store will work fine. Do not use a brush with plastic bristles, as it will melt.

## Fusing Wax Layers

Fusing your wax can be done in many ways for differing effects. Some of the most common tools are a heat gun, propane torch, or a small iron, but you can try any heat source that will get the wax back to its liquid form. You could even try a strong light bulb or setting your work outside on a sunny day!

1. Heat gun   2. Hake brush   3. Hog bristle brush   4. Quilting iron
5. Tacking iron   6. Propane torch   7. Scraping tools

## Adding Texture

Interesting effects can be achieved by pressing everyday items into the warm wax. Try using sticks, cookie cutters, or even rubber stamps. Just press these tools into the wax while it is soft but not liquid and experiment to see what effects you like.

## Revealing layers

Once you have built up several layers of wax, try scraping away areas that you have already fused to reveal what lies beneath. Pottery tools work well for this, but you can also get good effects with razor blades, paint scrapers and trowels.

## Using Stencils and Masks

These can be cut out of many materials including paper or heavy plastic. The trick to using them is to apply your encaustic paint, then fuse the wax with the stencil or mask still in place. This will keep your design from migrating while you heat it.

## Accenting Surface Marks

You can make surface marks in the wax with jar lids, computer parts or by drawing directly into the wax. These marks can be accented with oil paint or pastels to give a unique look that can't be achieved with wax alone.

**Find more techniques and projects at www.embracingencaustic.com**

## "Why Should You Mix Your Own?"

It is quick and convenient to purchase ready-made encaustic medium, but many artists mix their own. They often prefer more or less resin than is available in standard mixes, and it is much more cost effective if you plan to use large quantities of wax.

Most artists use two basic ingredients to make encaustic medium; beeswax and damar (da-MAHR) resin. Some artists prefer to add additional materials, but these two will get you started. I use a food scale to weigh out the materials first, and have them ready to go before I start mixing. It is always preferable have some form of ventilation available while mixing encaustic medium or paint, so open a door or put a fan in your window to draw any powder or fumes away from you just to be safe.

The resin, a type of hardened tree sap, comes in crystal form. Please note that damar resin is not the same thing as damar varnish, and the two are not interchangeable. For the following recipe, make sure you use damar resin.

# Making Encaustic Medium

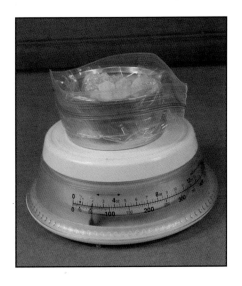

1. **Measure out your ingredients.** Start with one part of damar resin to eight parts of wax. This is a starting point, but you should experiment to get the ratio that works best for your style of painting. Once you get comfortable working with this ratio you may find you prefer to add a little more or less resin to your medium. The more damar, the harder the wax will be in the end. Don't add too much as the medium will be brittle. I try to stay within a range of 1:4 and 1:10 (resin:wax)

   Here's a handy mixing guide for a 1:8 ratio. Remember 1 pound = 16 oz.:

   | Resin | Wax |
   | --- | --- |
   | 1 oz. | 1/2 pound (8 oz.) |
   | 2 oz. | 1 pound |
   | 4 oz. | 2 pounds |
   | 8 oz. | 4 pounds |

2. **Melt a small amount of wax,** enough to cover the bottom of the pan, in order to get a true temperature reading. Heat to 150 degrees Fahrenheit (65 C.).

   *Be careful not to overheat the wax.* Wax has a flash point of around 450 degrees Fahrenheit (232 C.), above which it may catch on fire. If your wax is smoking, it's too hot. Always use a thermometer to be sure of your temperature. **Never leave melting wax unattended.**

3. **Add the resin** and raise the temperature to 200 – 225 degrees Fahrenheit (93 – 107 C.). Stir until melted and thoroughly mixed. It is normal for the resin to crackle and pop as it melts. Add the remaining wax and reduce the temperature to 175 degrees Fahrenheit (79 C.) until all the ingredients are melted and well mixed.

4. **Strain the mixture** while pouring it into individual muffin tins to cool. I use a kitchen strainer with some silkscreen material stretched over the mesh to remove extra fine particles. After the wax cools, put the whole tin in the freezer for 20 minutes, then flip the pan, and the cakes will pop right out! If you plan to buy new equipment for making your encaustic medium, consider splurging on silicone muffin pans. You'll never have to freeze them to get the wax out as they are flexible enough to peel off of the cakes when they are cool. If you already have metal tins, you can buy individual silicone cups to put inside them to get the same convenience.

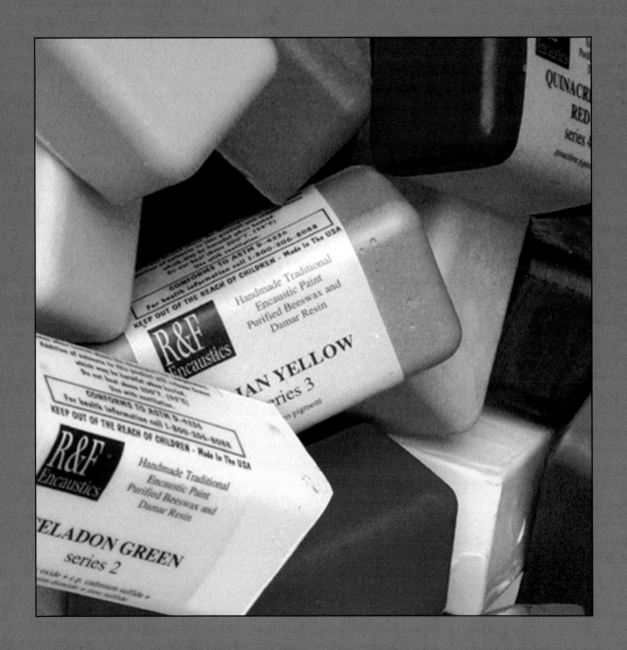

## Paint Options

Many artists prefer to buy their paint from trusted companies such as Evans Encaustics, Enkaustikos, R&F Handmade Paints or Wagner Encaustics. The expense of ready-made encaustic paints can be prohibitive, but it ensures evenness of color and consistency. Even if you buy your paint professionally mixed, you'll probably still want to add some encaustic medium to prepare different concentrations from more opaque versions to glazes.

It is also easy to make your own paint using beeswax, resin and pigment as you'll see on the following pages.

So which should you use, professionally mixed paint or paint you mix yourself? That answer depends on your budget and your need for consistency and evenness of color. Personally, I use both. I make my own medium and mix paint to suit my mood, but I also purchase the exceptionally beautiful paint available from all the paint makers listed above. They are hard to resist.

# Dry Pigments

Making your own paint can be a satisfying experience. Dry pigments are available in most art stores in an array of colors that won't break the bank. The trick here is to balance savings with safety as most powdered pigment, if mishandled, can be hazardous to your health.

### Safety Tips

- Do not work near a draft or fan that will blow pigments around.
- Wear a dust mask while handling pigments.
- Protect your skin from exposure by wearing gloves or using barrier cream.
- Keep your hands away from your face, especially your eyes

# Mixing with Dry Pigments

1. **Melt some encaustic medium into a container** or directly onto the griddle if you prefer.

2. **After you put on your gloves and dust mask,** dip your brush into the medium, then immediately into the bottle of pigment while the wax is still warm. The brush should be damp but not dripping. This way the pigment powder will have something to stick to while being moved into the medium.

3. **Carefully mix the powder into the encaustic medium** without spilling it on your skin or clothes. Mix well using your brush, and you're ready to paint! The specific amount of pigment and medium isn't too important. Just blend the two until you have paint that is the consistency and color you want.

# Professionally Mixed Paint

As I've mentioned, I use different brands of encaustic paint for different reasons. Here's a handy list of the major brands and why I love them:

### Evans Encaustics
www.evansencaustics.com

In addition to beautiful paint, I love Evans paint sticks in "fancy" colors that include metallic and duochrome colors. They also make grounds and top coats compatible with wax (Holy Grail, High Shine and Crack!)

Colors shown here: Bright Silver and Cloisonné Pink

### Enkaustikos! Wax Art Supplies
www.fineartstore.com

Enkaustikos offers 1 oz trial sizes of paint which are affordable enough to try a whole range of colors instead of buying just a few in larger quantities. They also have an extensive array of heated tools for painting with wax including pens and irons.

Photo credit: David Hoffend

### R&F Handmade Paints

www.rfpaints.com

I love the evenness and consistency of R&F paint as well as the extensive color choices—more than 80 at last count! They also offer exceptional pigment sticks that match many of their paint colors.

### Wagner Encaustics

www.wagnerencaustics.com

Aside from a variety of fun colors, Wagner is the only brand that comes packaged in a tin, ready to put right on the griddle so you can get painting. The metal caps are great for mixing small amounts of color.

## Using Stencils and Masks

You can use a variety of materials to mask off and protect one area of your work while working on another. Stencils and masks can be made from materials as simple as masking tape, but be sure to try other options such as frisket, fabric, cheesecloth, metal or mat board.

1. **Identify the area of the painting you want to mask off** and cover it with an appropriate material. For this example, I'll use ordinary masking tape, which works best on cool wax with a smooth surface.

2. **Burnish the tape down well to be sure it has good contact with your wax**, especially on the edges. You can use the tape to make a straight line, or use a sharp knife to cut a pattern into the edge of it. It's best to cut this pattern while the tape is on the wax so the line you cut will also score the wax, helping to keep the new layer of wax in place.

**Elise Wagner, Neutrino Pass**

2006, Encaustic on birch panel, 40" x 40"

"First I iron tracing or vellum paper onto the surface of the painting. I draw my shape onto the paper with a marker then hand cut the stencil with a utility knife, cutting into the wax at the same time. Before applying wax I burnish the paper, further securing it to prevent the wax from seeping under the stencil."

**Linda Womack, Altering the Path**

2007, Encaustic, hand made paper, material, oil paint, pastel on wood panel, 13" x 16"

"I applied thin strokes of oil paint to the first layer of wax and let it dry. The collage was made up of patterned paper, a page from a 19th century Japanese receipt book, fabric and encaustic paint. I used tape to form the diagonal line, and cut a mask out of cheesecloth in the shape of a bird to protect the colors beneath. The edges of the bird mask and the area representing a wing were painted with white wax in order to give texture to the outline of the image. I used a ceramics tool to incise wavy lines into the wax then highlighted them with white pastel before fusing lightly."

3. **Once your line is cut**, paint the new layer of wax over the cut edge of the tape and fuse the wax with the tape still in place.

4. **You'll need to watch the wax carefully** to see when to pull up the tape. If you do it too soon, the molten wax will spread past your masking line. If you wait too long, you might pull up more wax than you want to when the tape comes up. When you first fuse the wax it will be shiny and as it cools it will start to cloud. Wait for that cloudy state before carefully pulling up your tape.

5. **Once the tape is off**, you can clean up any edges that spilled over using a small scraping tool or a razor blade. Because you fused this wax with the mask in place, you shouldn't need to fuse it again unless you want to soften the edges of your masked area.

# Incising Lines

1. **Paint and fuse at least four layers of wax onto your surface**, using any colors you want as your background. The more layers you start with, the easier it is to get a deep enough line carved in your wax to practice this technique. In the example below I started with 6 layers of wax.

2. **Carve out a design in your wax**, taking care not to go all the way through to the original board unless that is your goal. Carefully scrape away any raised edges left by the incising, using a palette knife or a scraping tool.

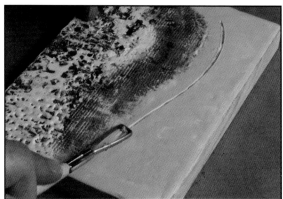

**Janet Bartlett Goodman, Down the Road (Diptych)**

2007, Encaustic and oil stick on wood panel, 26" x 36" (cropped to fit page)

"Several layers of encaustic wax were layered and fused. I incised the lines into the surface using calligraphy pens and pottery tools (needle, loop & ribbon tools). Sparingly, I use a ravioli cutter! Oil stick was rubbed into the incised line and any excess can be removed with vegetable oil."

*or other pigment*

3. **Dab hot wax into the line you just created** and let it cool for 30 seconds. IMPORTANT: Do not fuse this new layer of wax until you do the next step!

4. **Use a scraping tool to gently remove the wax** that did not fill the incised line. This should leave you with a well defined line in the shape that you originally scraped into the wax.

5. **Optional: Heat the filled wax line very gently**, just until it gets shiny, to ensure it is fused to the rest of your wax.

**Andrea Benson, Jump/Snake**

2004, Encaustic with paper and Xerox on wood panel, 12" x 17"

"The grass was incised with a linoleum tool that has a V-shaped blade, then the lines were filled with wax. The figure and snake were built-up off the surface in low relief. I smoothed and carved the melted wax edges with small woodcut tools after each fusing to get a clean sculpted surface."

**Gregory Wright, Diverted Expectations**

2007, Encaustic and oil on wood panel, 24" x 24"

"Lines of different widths and depths were incised into the wax using a variety of scratch board nibs and a utility knife. I applied oil bars and oil paints mixed with a little linseed oil to the incised lines, then wiped away the excess leaving just the filled line visible."

**Mary Farmer, Ambrosia Morning**

2008, Encaustic, paper, watercolor, raw pigment and oil stick on panel, 30" x 22"

"I use print making needles to incise thin lines into the wax. Using gloves, I tap a small amount of raw pigment into my hand and rub it into the surface (use a mask and good ventilation). For wider lines I use wood carving tools and usually fill those incisions with a hand made oil stick (Equal parts oil paint, linseed oil and beeswax) and wipe away the excess."

# Revealing Layers

1. **Build up layers of color and texture in a random pattern on your board.** Try to work in both warm and cool colors for the best effect. I prefer organic shapes, but this technique will work with any shape or pattern you like. Try dripping the wax on in different directions to get more variation. Fuse well, then let this layer cool for a few minutes before continuing to the next step.

2. **Using a thick, opaque wax for this layer will yield the best results.** Paint over the previous layers of wax, completely covering them with this new layer of paint. Fuse without disturbing the layers of wax below.

**Jeff Juhlin, Bysect**

2007, Encaustic on wood panel, 20" x 20"

"After building up layers of wax, I used a carpenter's awl to incise lines deeply into the surface of the work. I incised the lines nearly down to the panel, exposing the many layers and colors beneath the top layer of translucent wax."

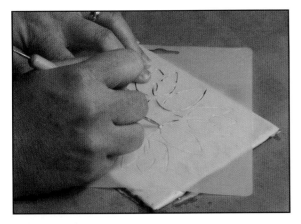

**3. Once this layer has cooled** but is not completely cold, scrape off parts of the opaque layer of wax to reveal the colors and textures beneath. There are several ways to do this:

- Scraping parts of the upper layers with sharp tools like trowels, ceramics tools, or even a screwdriver can reveal additional layers.

- Lay a stencil on top of your cool wax. Scrape off the top layer of wax through the openings to reveal the color beneath in the pattern of the stencil.

Scraping in broad strokes directly on the uneven wax can also reveal layers below in an interesting way. Try turning your board and scraping from all directions for maximum effect.

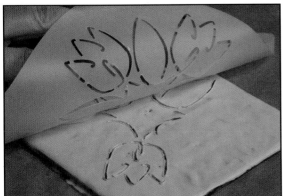

**Linda Womack, Dream in Shadow**

2007, Encaustic, joint compound, pastel on wood panel, 13" x 13"

"I applied joint compound directly to a wood panel and let it dry, then sealed it with a layer of encaustic medium. After masking off the diagonal line with tape, I added several layers of encaustic paint in contrasting colors then finished with a coat of white paint. I scraped back through the layers to reveal different colors and shapes. To finish the green area on top, I incised lines and highlighted them with white pastel before fusing lightly."

# Image Transfer

Make a black and white photocopy of the image you want to transfer onto regular-weight paper. Inkjet prints will not work for this technique, as it's the toner from the copy that transfers onto the wax. Black and white laser prints will work, because they are toner based. Remember, transfers come out backward. If you want to use text make sure your words are reversed on your photocopy.

1. **Paint a base of at least two layers of wax** onto your board and fuse each layer. A very smooth finish will get you the best transferred image.

2. **Place the print face down on your wax.** Burnish it with a spoon to get a good connection between the toner and the wax.

**Marybeth Rothman, Specified Sequence**

2005, Encaustic, charcoal transfer, oil paint stick, charcoal pencil drawing on acid free paper, photograph, on birch wood panel, 12" x 12"

"I used a charcoal transfer to create the grid and marks on my image. After coating tracing paper with vine charcoal, I placed it charcoal side down on a warm encaustic surface. I drew lines on the clean side of the paper to transfer the charcoal to the wax, then I peeled the paper off and carefully fused the surface. Collage and incising techniques were also used."

3. **Dab the back of your image** with nail polish remover to release the toner from the paper, transferring your image onto the wax. You should be able to see the image through the back of the paper, but using too much solvent may cause your image to smear or run.

4. **After the transfer dries**, fuse it gently with a heat gun then coat it with a layer of encaustic medium to seal it into your work.

**Linda Womack, Strength Comes**

2007, Encaustic, image transfer, inkjet photograph, raw pigment on Claybord™, 6" x 6"

"I sealed my board with encaustic medium first, then applied water with raw pigment and used a propane torch to fuse. This leaves a beaded pattern of the water as a mark in the wax. I added the architectural image as a solvent transfer, using polish remover to release the toner from the paper. The color image is an inkjet print on tissue paper collaged in with wax. I added blue encaustic paint as an accent to finish the piece."

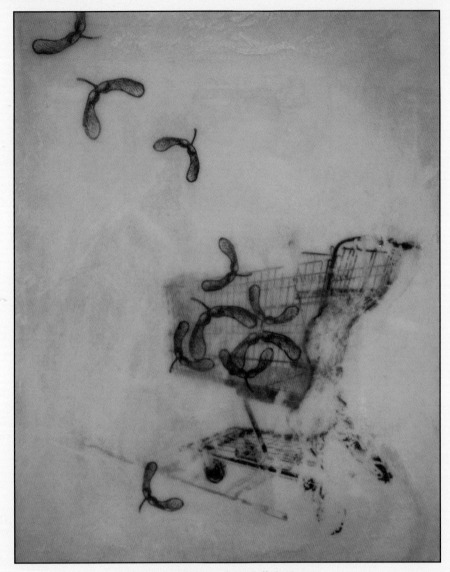

**Tracy Spadafora, Cart Full-O-Nature**

2001, Encaustic, transfer on Claybord™, 12" x 9"

"I started with a layer of muted yellow encaustic paint, then fused with a heat gun to a smooth surface. The first transfer was a black & white photocopy of a shopping cart transfered directly onto the surface by rubbing with water. I fused it with a heat gun to distort it a little then coated it with encaustic medium to seal it. The maple seed images were transfered in the same way. The layer of medium in between the shopping cart and the maple seeds creates depth in the painting."

**Bridgette Guerzon Mills, Creve Coeur**

2008, Encaustic, photocopy, cheesecloth, and thread on wood, 6" x 6"

"I coated the wood panel with encaustic medium then made an image transfer directly onto the wax. A black and white photocopy was placed facedown and burnished onto the wax. After wetting the image, the paper pulp was rolled off leaving nothing but the photograph on the wax. Sewn pieces of cheesecloth were adhered using encaustic medium to finish the piece."

**Amber George, Parasol Landscape**

2006, Encaustic, dictionary pages, photocopies and china marker on birch panel, 42" x 21"

"I used dictionary pages dipped in wax and fused to the waxed surface of the panel with a quilting iron. The solid black areas are photocopies of the plant, adhered in the same fashion as the dictionary pages. Painted areas were built up using simple brush work. I used a china marker for the more delicate line work, then lightly fused it into the wax."

# Collage with Wax

When you collage items into your projects, the type of materials you choose will determine the technique you should use.

## Thin or Porous Materials

Materials like tissue paper, dress patterns, paper towels, patterned napkins, light weight fabric and dried plants can be added by painting clear medium right over the top of them and fusing well.

1. **In the case of delicate materials like leaves and flowers**, paint "with the grain" following the structure of the plant. Doing so will ensure that the plant lies naturally in the collage.

2. **When using images that are stamped or printed onto thin paper**, the white areas will disappear leaving only the stamped image or the other colors in the pattern visible. This gives a wonderful effect! The example here uses a patterned napkin.

## Thicker Materials

Thicker materials require a little more preparation. Regular-weight computer paper, scrapbook paper, heavy-weight material, or light weight three dimensional materials can all be incorporated into your wax.

1. **For computer paper or anything heavier**, coat the paper with clear encaustic medium first to keep from trapping air bubbles between the wax and the paper when fusing. Lay the paper down directly on the griddle and brush on the medium. If the piece is small enough you can dip it directly into the wax. Then place it onto your collage before the wax cools and fuse lightly.

2. **If some areas don't stick**, use a small iron to tack the paper back down. Once the paper is secure and there are no air bubbles, cover the paper surface with a thin layer of encaustic medium to seal in the paper and fuse.

**Judith Williams, Passage**

2007, Encaustic, oil, collage on wood panel, 24" x 24"

"Patterned collage papers and thin Asian calligraphy papers were glued with acrylic gel medium onto a surface of joint compound. Thin oil paint strokes were applied and layers of wax were added."

**Linda Cordner, Hybrid 6**

2007, Encaustic, oil, paper on wood panel, 12" x 12"

"I printed the design on rice paper using an inkjet printer, then cut it out and laid it on on the red wax. I covered it with a clear layer of encaustic medium and fused lightly. The shapes in the white area were painted with clear wax, then I filled the texture with black oil stick and buffed off the excess."

**Bridgette Guerzon Mills, Remembering**

2007, Encaustic, inkjet photograph and lace on wood, 8" x 8"

"I printed a color photograph of the tree and adhered it to the wood panel with encaustic medium, adding multiple colors of encaustic paint to create the ground and sky. I embedded a piece of lace into the wax and then inscribed lines with a sharp tool to add texture."

# Adding Texture

*random, organic texture?*

*How many ways to start with a)*

Part of the lure of working in wax is the sculptural quality inherent in the material, especially when you manipulate the surface. Adding texture is one of my favorite reasons to paint using encaustic. There are many ways to add or enhance existing texture, but I'll show you the basics here.

1. **It is much easier to build up texture on a surface that is already a bit rough**. In this example I scuffed up my wax with an ordinary trowel from the hardware store. Since trowels aren't very sharp, scrape the surface while your wax is a little soft.

2. **Once you have the wax roughed up, dip your brush in clear medium and wait about 30 seconds before brushing it on**, in order to let the wax cool a little. When you apply the wax, do it at an extreme angle as shown here, so the wax only ends up on the higher ridges. Fuse gently. You can use pigmented wax for this step, but I find the first coat can be quite messy, so I use clear medium. Any mistakes are less obvious and easier to clean up.

**Elizabeth Back, O Three**

2007, Encaustic and oil on panel, 20" x 20"

"I build the edges of the craters by embedding a clay ball mold, dripping and painting wax around the balls with approximately 10 layers of wax. I remove the ball to reveal the layers and depth of the surface, scraping back then adding more wax. I incise with a needle tool or a pen, then add oil paint to enhance the lines and texture."

**3. For the rest of the layers, choose whatever colors you like.** Use the same technique as in the previous step, letting your brush cool before applying your wax. Be sure to turn your board, and brush the wax on from all different angles to build up high relief.

Here are examples of what the layers look like at 4, 8 and 12 layers of wax. Notice how adding a contrasting color near the top emphasizes the texture.

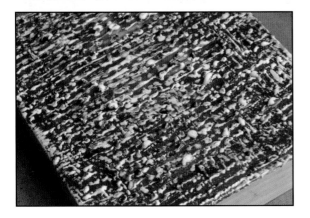

**Linda Womack, Always in Season**

2007, Encaustic, joint compound, gold leaf on Claybord™, 16" x 16"

"I applied joint compound directly to my panel to create the leaves and the mountains and let it dry. I sealed that with a layer of encaustic medium and continued building up the image with smooth layers encaustic paint. I added texture by dragging a cool brush over the wax surface, or painting through cheesecloth. As a last step gold leaf was added to emphasize the leaf that is the focal point of the painting."

**Diana Gonzalez Gandolfi, Lost**

2005, Encaustic, wood strips and oil on wood, 32" x 28"

"Wood strips were glued to a birch panel and coated with encaustic paint. After incising, oil paint was rubbed and wiped on the lower surface areas then scraped with a utility blade to reveal additional textures. I applied masking and stenciling techniques using wax paper, masking tape and Plasticine. The wax was poured in stages, and hand-cut stencils made of frosted mylar were used to paint the white balloon shape and other images."

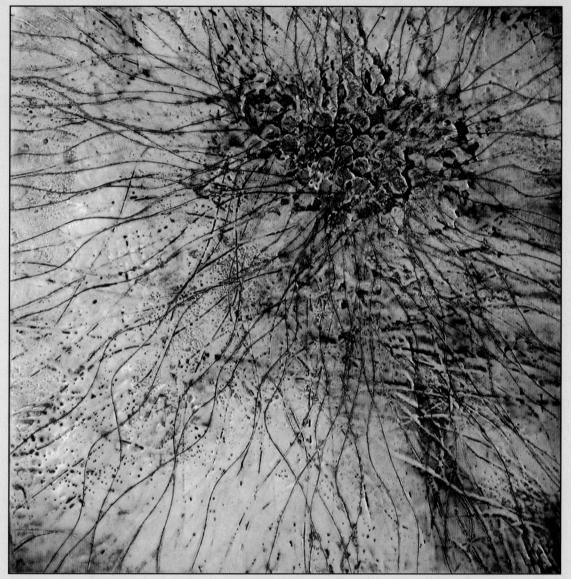

**Jeff Juhlin, Regeneration #1**

2006, Encaustic and oil on wood panel, 12" x 12"

"I used a section of perforated steel sheeting and poured the wax through the holes to create the central cluster of this piece. I then built up layers of wax around the cluster and incised the flagella like tentacles that emanated from the cluster."

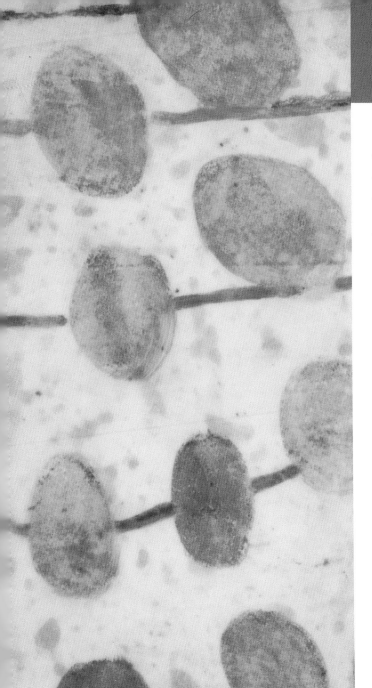

The art you'll see in this section reflects work that uses the properties of painting with wax and the techniques presented here to their best effect. Some of these artists use techniques that are beyond the scope of this book, but I hope their work will serve as inspiration for you to continue exploring this exciting medium.

All of the artists represented throughout the book have been gracious enough to allow me to share their work with you, and for that I am grateful. *Embracing Encaustic* wouldn't be nearly as interesting without these talented painters. Their contact information, including web sites when available, can be viewed at www. embracingencaustic.com. I hope you will contact them and thank them for their contribution!

### Diana Gonzalez Gandolfi, *Returning (Diptych)*

2007, Encaustic monotype mounted on board, 12" x 21" (cropped on right panel)

"This one-of-a-kind encaustic print was pulled from wax applied to a warm metal plate and then mounted on to a board. The images in this print were created by layering images rather than by a single pass. To create the rocks on the left panel, wax paper stencils, previously coated with dense encaustic color, were placed on top of a warm plate (150 degrees) and printed over a previously pulled image using a barren and a etching burnisher to apply pressure. The right panel was created by double printing, each time changing the intensity and transparency of the color."

Photo Credit: Greg Leshé

### Kevin Frank, Red Escalator

2007, Encaustic on panel, 18" x 24"

"I draw an outline of my subject, in graphite or charcoal, directly onto the panel before sealing it with encaustic medium with a tint of color. With the under-drawing visible, I block in the mass tones, alla prima, using straight encaustic paint with no medium added. I make adjustments to the form by using several metal tools including a small, spoon-shaped cuticle-pushing tool, which I usually heat first and a small pocket knife for scraping and incising. Sometimes to achieve more subtle shading, I use my thumb or forefinger to blend the tones. Typically, I use hog bristle brushes for large areas and small sable brushes for the fine details."

**Sue Roberts, Safe Voyage**

2006, Painted clay and encaustic, 18" x 23" x 8"

"Clear encaustic medium is brushed over the painted clay surface, then fused with a heat gun to eliminate brush strokes. It is time consuming to brush the melted wax on to a dimensional and detailed surface, but I love the translucency, depth and lifelike feel encaustic brings to the finished painted clay figure."

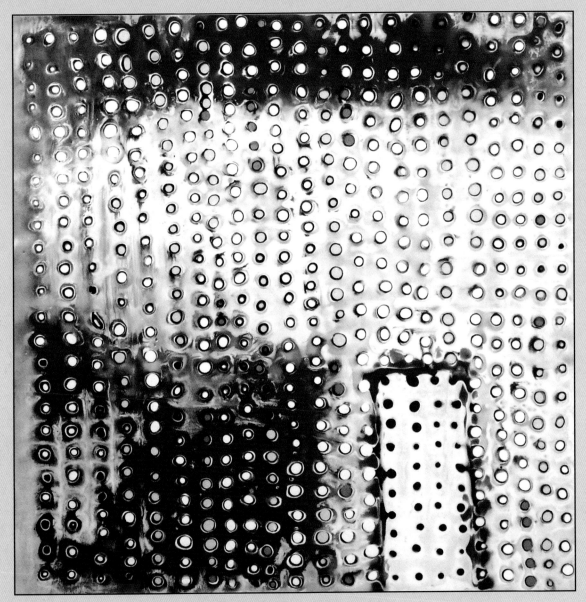

**Eileen P. Goldenberg, Tea House #220**

2007, Encaustic on wood panel, 12" x 12"

"The meditation of painting thousands of dots of wax begins each painting. After building up many layers of wax, I scrape back the surface, an archeological process of excavation. Sections of mostly layers of clear wax utilize the translucency of the material and give a view of underlying layers."

**Paula Roland, Bounce**

2007, Encaustic, pigment, graphite on handmade Korean paper, 15" x 13.5"

"Heavy handmade paper was dipped repeatedly in white encaustic paint, then painted on with a mixture of powdered graphite and denatured alcohol. Additional marks were made using graphite transfer paper and lines were incised into the wax using a loop ceramic tool. The piece was fused with a 600 watt light bulb and a heat gun."

**Elise Wagner, Particle Sphere**

2008, Encaustic on birch panel, 60" x 48" (courtesy Butters Gallery, LTD)

"This piece consists of several layers of wax that was ironed onto the birch panel with various incised lines and shapes. A wax pen was used to make the white diagonal lines, while the circular pattern on the left was painted freehand and scraped back."

**Alicia Tormey, Delicate Balance**

2007, Encaustic, oil on wood panel, 24" x 32"

"The fine lines were created by incising the surface and rubbing oil paint into the grooves. A new layer of wax was then fused over each line to seal the mark. I created the marble effect on the left by alternating layers of shellac, wax and oil paint and then using a torch to shift the surface of each layer."

**Scott Reilly, The Construction of Thought**

2008, Encaustic on Plexiglas illuminated with fluorescents, 48" x 48"

(Left: instillation view from Hayes Valley Market Gallery)

"When using Plexiglas the biggest problem is adhesion, so I rough up the plexi with a sander first. Sometimes I drill small holes into it as well, giving the wax one more surface to grab on to. I also embed sheets of fiberglass into the layers of wax, giving it another porous material to latch on to and adding a textural element to my work that is fibrous and organic."

**Andrea Benson, Glyphs Raining**

2004, Encaustic on wood panel with paper, Xerox, feathers and lace, 17" x 12"

"Art paper highlighted with colored pencil makes up the umbrella and dress, then bits of old lace were added. The face is a small photocopy of a photograph, drawn on first with colored pencil to highlight some features. Colored wax was added to build up the face and visually connect it with the body. The hair is composed of small feathers."

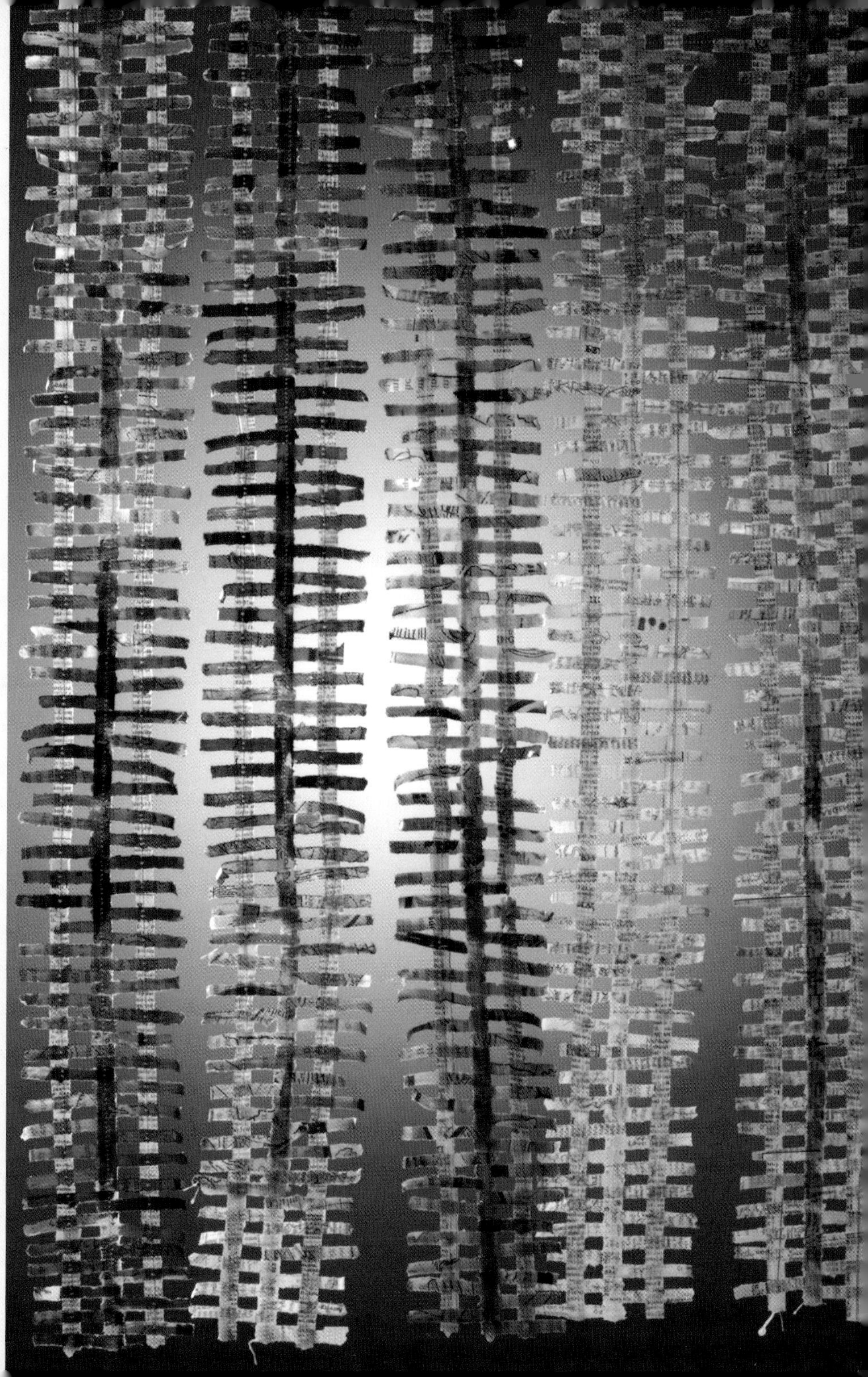

**Daniella Woolf, Shelter**

2006

Encaustic, thread,
dictionary pages, painted
text, maps, 18" x 12"

"I glue shreds of paper to a central
spine, then sew the shredded
elements to the spine. I then dip
them in encaustic medium, which
renders the paper translucent.
I prefer my works to hang in space
so that both sides are revealed."

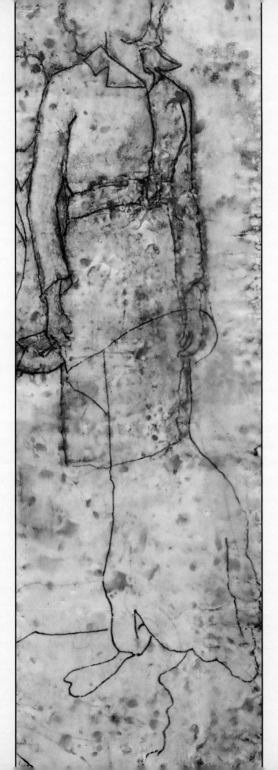

**Natasia Chan, Pull**

2007, Encaustic, ink on plaster prepared canvas
on panel, 21" x 7"

"I wrapped and glued the canvas to the cradled
substrate with PVA glue and staples on the back.
Once the glue was dry, I spread Aglaia Marvelizing
Surfacer (made with marble powder) onto the
canvas. I let the plaster cure for a few hours, then
I sanded to a smooth white surface and sealed
it with encaustic medium. I created a mottled
ground by splattering cyan and magenta encaustic
paint and then painting the whole surface white
and scraping back to reveal the colors beneath. The
lines were made with a trace monotype in which I
made my own "carbon paper" using etching ink
applied to wax paper that has been allowed to dry
overnight to a "tacky" consistency. I used a brush
with walnut oil to soften the line and blot excess oil
with newsprint. I only used one color per layer with
clear medium in between to preserve the layers."

**Janet Bartlett Goodman, Sam**

2005, Encaustic, color pencils, oil paint, watercolor, rice paper, oil stick,
on cradled Claybord™, 24" x 24"

"Most of the background is painted and drawn directly on the panel using watercolor and pencils. Nine pieces of rice paper were used, with a photograph of Sam's face printed onto one. The body was painted and drawn on to another. The rice paper is pulled through encaustic medium and adhered to the panel. The rice paper becomes transparent so the under painting on the panel becomes visible. Oil stick is rubbed over the whole piece and another layer of encaustic medium is applied and fused."

**Tracy Spadafora, Cycle of Growth**

2005, Encaustic, paper and oil on braced luan, 16" x 16"

"Schematic maps of artery projects were adhered directly onto the support panel. A very thick coat of encaustic medium was applied to the maps and smoothed out with a tacking iron. Images of flowers were created by etching lines into the encaustic medium and filling them in with encaustic paint and oil paint. Thin glazes of oil paint were also applied over the encaustic medium surface."

**Linda Womack, Above and Beyond**

2007, Encaustic, inkjet photograph, raw pigment on Claybord™, 8" x 8"

"I sealed the panel with encasutic medium, then applied water with raw pigment and used a propane torch to fuse. This leaves a pattern of the water as a mark in the wax, colored by the pigment. The image is an inkjet print on tissue paper of my own photograph which I then collaged in with clear encaustic medium."

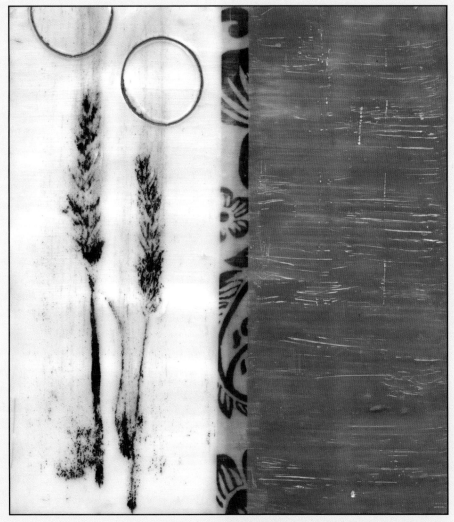

**Amy Stoner, Foxtail Moon**

2008, Encaustic, art paper, oil paint, carbon paper, 7" x 6"

"After applying white paint on the left and variations of green and white on the right, I highlighted some rough brush strokes with white oil paint. A thin strip of art paper added a bold dividing line between the sections. The foxtails were created by tracing an image laid over black carbon paper, which transferred the carbon onto the wax. A layer of encaustic medium protects the carbon drawing. Small circles were incised then filled with orange oil paint."

## Encaustic Paint & Wax Suppliers

**Dadant & Sons**
(888) 922-1293
www.dadant.com/catalog/
Natural and clear beeswax

**Enkaustikos! Wax Art Supplies**
(800) 836-8940
www.fineartstore.com
Wax, resin, medium, paint, specialty tools

**Hylla Evans**
www.evansencaustics.com
728 First Street West, Sonoma, CA
Encaustic paint, medium, grounds, top coats

**R&F Handmade Paints**
(800) 206-8088
www.rfpaints.com
Wax, resin, paint, tools

**Wagner Encaustics, Inc.**
www.wagnerencaustics.com
Encaustic paint, medium

## Pigments

**Earth Pigments**
(520) 682-8928
www.earthpigments.com
Non-toxic, natural pigments

**Sinopia Pigments & Materials**
321 Seventh St, San Francisco, CA
www.sinopia.com
Pigments, encaustic tools, books

**Williamsburg**
(800) 293-9399
www.williamsburgoilpaint.bizland.com
Dry pigments, oil paint, art supplies

Photo credit: David Hoffend

Enkaustikos Mini Palette Knife

## Art Panels

**Ampersand Art**
(800) 822-1939
www.ampersandart.com
Claybord™ art panels

**Art Boards**
(800) 546-7985
www.art-boards.com
Archival wood art panels

**Art Substrates**
www.artsubstrates.com
Panels, float frames and custom art grounds

**Custom Art Panels**
www.rodneythompson.com
Cradled panels and specialty art panels

## Learn More

**Embracing Encaustic Web Site**
www.embracingencaustic.com
Tips, projects, workshops

**R&F Paints Forum**
rfpaints.com/forum/
Technical forum and calls for art

## Artist Organizations

**International Encaustic Artists**
www.international-encaustic-artists.org

**New England Wax**
www.newenglandwax.org

**Texas Wax**
Dallas: texaswaxdallas.blogspot.com
Houston: ancientvessel-degrees.blogspot.com

## Reference Books

*The Art of Encaustic Painting*
www.joannemattera.com
By Joanne Mattera

*Encaustic & Beyond: A Guide To Creating Fine Art With Wax*
By Lissa Rankin
Published by Sterling Publishing in 2009

*Enkaustikos! Wax Art*
www.fineartstore.com
By Ann Huffman

# About the Authors

**Linda Womack** is an artist and art instructor living in Portland, Oregon. Her work has been shown in galleries throughout the United States. Linda shares her love of encaustic painting through books, blogs and live workshops and has been featured on Home & Garden Television (HGTV). She is the founder of the Oregon chapter of the International Encaustic Artists and was a featured speaker at the National Encaustic Conference in 2008. Find out more about her art, workshops and blog on her web site at www.lindawomack.com.

Linda's other half, **William Womack**, is a writer and designer. He is currently penning his second novel, *Last Thursday*, a tale of murder and intrigue set against the backdrop of the Portland arts scene. His thoughts on writing and the writing life can be found at www.wordsforwriters.com.

To order additional copies of *Embracing Encaustic*, visit

www.embracingencaustic.com or call (503) 348-9139

Our web site offers inspiration,
project ideas, and additional information
on the artists profiled in this book.